# Conversations
# on the Hudson

# Conversations on the Hudson

An Englishman
bicycles five hundred
miles through
the Hudson Valley,
meeting artists
and craftspeople
along the way

Nick Hand

PRINCETON ARCHITECTURAL PRESS · NEW YORK

Published by Princeton Architectural Press
37 East Seventh Street, New York, New York 10003
Visit our website at www.papress.com

The Department of Small Works Editor: Harriet Hand
Princeton Architectural Press Editor: Sara Bader
Design: The Department of Small Works
Photography: Nick Hand
Illustrations: Jon McNaught
Photograph of Woody Guthrie: Al Aumuller
Transcripts have been edited from original recordings and printed
with the kind permission of their authors.

Special thanks to: Meredith Baber, Nicola Bednarek Brower,
Janet Behning, Megan Carey, Carina Cha, Andrea Chlad, Barbara Darko,
Benjamin English, Russell Fernandez, Will Foster, Tessa Hartley,
Jan Hartman, Jan Haux, Diane Levinson, Jennifer Lippert,
Katharine Myers, Lauren Palmer, Margaret Rogalski, Elana Schlenker,
Rob Shaeffer, Sara Stemen, Andrew Stepanian, Paul Wagner, and
Joseph Weston of Princeton Architectural Press—Kevin C. Lippert, publisher

Library of Congress Cataloging-in-Publication Data:
Hand, Nick.
 Conversations on the Hudson / Nick Hand. — First Edition.
   pages cm
 Includes index.
 ISBN 978-1-61689-224-1
1. Artisans—Hudson River Valley (N.Y. and N.J.)—Interviews. 2. Industries—
Hudson River Valley (N.Y. and N.J.) 3. Hand, Nick—Travel—Hudson River
Valley (N.Y. and N.J.) I. Title.
 NK1411.5.H36 2014
 745.09747'3—dc23
                    2013013839

To Pete Seeger, who stood up and sang
the songs that needed to be heard
and launched the sloop *Clearwater*
to save the Hudson River.

# Table of Contents

# Introduction

The river is shrouded in cloud as I bike down the valley. Big river, huge sky, gentle hills. Alive with birdsong like I've never heard before. Towns doing well; towns doing not so well. Along a path through the woods and on, with the weight of a heavily laden English touring bicycle, I roll down a loose gravel hill slightly out of control. I search out the River Road. I've found that anything called River Road in the Hudson Valley is generally quiet and tree-lined, a dappled sunlit road that at some point will open to wonderful river views.

My home is Bristol, a small city in the southwest of England. At the start of last year my wife, Harriet, worked in New York City for six months, which gave me the perfect opportunity to indulge in my very favorite pastime, a long bicycle ride, and one that gave me the chance to seek out interesting folk. For some years, I've been recording the work of artisans around Britain and have been inspired by the makers' enlightened view on life. They learn a skill and make beautiful things, in a slow, considered way. The bicycle seems to bring out the best in people, not just me. I meet great people, with a good story to tell to a passing cyclist.

I arrived in New York City with my trusty Argos bicycle and started the ride from our temporary front door in Brooklyn, crossing the East River and Manhattan Island to set out north along the mighty Hudson River toward Hudson Falls.

On a bicycle you take everything in, you can stop anywhere, you don't miss a thing, and it's easy to strike up a conversation. A chance meeting in Rockland County is a fine example. I met Ted Ludwiczak at the end of a lovely ride through the wooded Nyack Beach State

Park. Ted's house was pretty much the first one built in the village of Haverstraw. A wooden painted building, typical except for the rows of carved stone faces looking out to the street. A red car rolled up and Ted appeared, a brilliant old boy who told me his story over the next couple of hours. His daughter came by later and said how unusual it was for Ted to open up to people. I put it down to arriving by bicycle and not being in any kind of hurry.

I was already aware of the connection between this part of the world and Woody Guthrie, a personal hero of mine. At the start of the journey I had detoured in Manhattan to pay tribute to Joe Strummer, at his memorial mural on Seventh Street and Avenue A. Joe, who died ten years ago, was best known as the singer in the Clash, and at one point had called himself "Woody," after Woody Guthrie. Later on in my journey, I was really chuffed to meet Anna Canoni, Woody Guthrie's granddaughter. I would also get to see Pete Seeger at a Clearwater tribute to Woody. Clearwater is a project set up by Pete in 1966 to save his beloved Hudson River from the effects of decades of industrial pollution. Pete is a legendary folksinger and activist, and has dedicated much of his long life to the Clearwater project. In 1969 he launched the sloop *Clearwater*, considered by many as America's environmental flagship.

The Hudson River is wide enough in parts to not quite make out features or landscape on the far side. It winds its way up to the state capital, Albany, and beyond, where it finally narrows as it continues toward Hudson Falls. Away from the river, the lanes and highways are lined with painted wooden buildings with blue plaques detailing its history; the Revolutionary War or sometimes pioneering incidents from earlier days. On my journey up the vast river with its majestic bridges I heard stories of times past: of lone sharks, shad, striped bass, catfish, and huge leaping sturgeon. A river overfished and polluted for much of its recent history. The river is in recovery and thanks to the work of Clearwater, it's gradually returning to its former glory.

The hills, mountains, and countryside are only partly tamed. Some areas, like the Catskills and the source of the river at Lake Tear of the Clouds in the Adirondack Mountains, are still wild in parts, where coyotes and black bears roam, and there are rattlesnakes and bald eagles and other huge birds of prey.

I snaked my way up the Hudson Valley on a five-hundred-mile journey using the guidance of Ken Roberts and his excellent Bike Hudson Valley website. I used Twitter as a kind of ongoing diary and wrote the occasional blog post. I recorded and photographed the people I was fortunate to meet along the route, and this book is a document of those remarkable artisans. I've let them tell their own stories. I hope that you're as inspired by their words as I was when I met them.

**Nick Hand**

SARATOGA

HUDSON FALLS

Carole Foster
SPINNER

NORTHUMBERLAND

Jordan Fruchter
MOSAICIST

SCHUYLERVILLE

RENSSELAER

Derek Grout
DISTILLER

ALBANY

Lee & Georgia Ranney
FARMERS

Julie Hedrick
PAINTER & POET

Peter Wetzler
COMPOSER & PIANIST

GREENE

COLUMBIA

VALATIE

Steve Clearman
MOTORCYCLE COLLECTOR

Tom Crowell
BREWER

CHATHAM

Deborah Ehrlich
GLASS DESIGNER

GHENT

LENOX

John & Janine Stockin
MAPLE SYRUP PRODUCERS

ULSTER

HUDSON

Michele O'Hana
CERAMICIST

Ken Greene
SEED LIBRARIAN

Nick Zachos
BOAT RESTORER

DUTCHESS

Timothy Ganon
YURT OWNER

KINGSTON

ACCORD

Luke Ives Pontifell
PRINTER & PUBLISHER

NEWBURGH

PUTNAM

ORANGE

WESTCHESTER

Ted Ludwiczak
SCULPTOR

HAVERSTRAW

MOUNT KISCO

Anna Canoni
WOODY GUTHRIE'S
GRANDDAUGHTER

ROCKLAND

Pasqualina Azzarello
BICYCLE RECYCLER

Thomas Wright &
Joseph Fratesi
DESIGNERS

Peter Buchanan-Smith
AXE RESTORER & MAKER

MANHATTAN

BROOKLYN
NEW YORK CITY

11

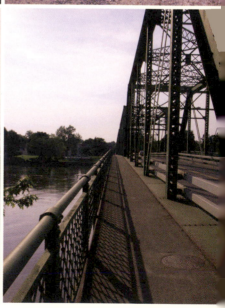

## Thomas Wright and Joseph Fratesi, Designers
### Brooklyn, New York City

**TW**: My name's Thomas Wright, and we're at the showroom of Atlas Industries, on Douglass Street in Brooklyn. My partner, Joseph Fratesi, and I are designers. We design just about anything.

**JF**: Designers, builders, inventors.

**TW**: It's funny, Joseph and I didn't start out intending to spearhead a handmade trend. This is just what makes sense to us. We're drawn to a certain level of honesty in the materials. A certain expression of how things are put together. These things just developed, not because we wanted to make a statement, but because that's what spoke to us and what's important to us.

Handmade things communicate something. People are reacting to a world dominated by manufactured products. Workers crank out manufactured products—which are essentially never touched by human hands—and after a while, people are hungry for things that they can react to on a more human level. They want to understand how the object is built, the materials used to make it, its real presence in the world—something that doesn't have planned obsolescence and will last as long as they want to take care of it and keep it going. They can pass it down to their kids. I'm really proud that our furniture falls into that category, something that people will hang onto and cherish for a long time.

Since we spend so much time staring at the computer, our lives generally exist in sort of a virtual sphere. I think that's another way in which people have developed a sense of longing for the physical world.

The iPhone is an incredible object, but people don't have any sense of how it's put together; they're not really asked to or allowed to understand how it's made.

**JF**: Ten years ago, there was a kind of exaltation of the manufactured product: a lot of plastics and knockdown furniture—it was a very different world. Now, people are beginning to appreciate that craft is more or less a dying thing, and there's a welcome resurgence. It most definitely has changed in the last ten years.

**TW**: As I said, we didn't set out to start a trend. This is how we wanted to do it. We were excited about something that we designed and we said, "OK, now we need to go build it with the tools that we have and in the way that we know how to do things, to create a beautiful object." We didn't think, "OK, we'll design something that's going to be manufactured and mass-produced, and what's the most expedient way to extract a profit margin from this whole process?" It was making something simply and, actually, the hard way. When we would talk to people ten or fifteen years ago, they would say, "That sounds like a really complex way of doing things." But it's the only way that makes sense to us.

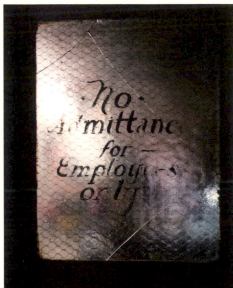

## Pasqualina Azzarello, Bicycle Recycler
### Brooklyn, New York City

My name is Pasqualina Azzarello, and I'm the executive director of Recycle-A-Bicycle.

It's very inspiring to have my office and my meetings here, to be surrounded by this very direct transformation that takes place with bicycles, with people, with students. Recycle-A-Bicycle has come a long way since its inception. It started seventeen years ago as a youth program of Transportation Alternatives, the primary advocacy organization in New York City for cyclists and pedestrians. Since then we've grown to include two retail stores in Brooklyn and Manhattan, a job-training center in Queens, and nine school-based programs across all five boroughs.

In addition to our locations, we do a number of community events, like Bike Bonanzas. We provide twenty-five refurbished bicycles and run volunteer events to repair kids' bikes. We bring them to public spaces throughout the city, usually parks, and host a bike swap. Parents donate the bicycles that no longer fit their children and we have mechanics on hand to refurbish the bikes that are coming in during the day. Then children can upgrade to a bicycle that fits. It's very sweet to see the little kids donate their bikes, and meet the younger ones who will now get to ride them.

People have so many different reasons for riding bicycles and it's important to recognize that in the work that we do. Whether it's the youth that come into Recycle-A-Bicycle or staff or community partners, there's room for everybody. That's a wonderful thing for someone to feel. We believe that if the streets are safer, more people of all ages will ride, and that's really what we want to see happen.

## Peter Buchanan-Smith, Axe Restorer and Maker
### Manhattan, New York City

My name is Peter Buchanan-Smith, and I'm the founder of Best Made Company.

In 2009 the economy tanked and the world seemed like it was coming to an end, so I decided to take matters into my own hands. I had the opportunity to contribute products to Andy Spade's store here in New York, and for whatever reason, I dipped deep into my childhood memory and pulled out an axe. I started painting the handles of them, as a sign of respect for this tool that I loved and that I felt was relevant at the time. Everything in the world seemed complicated and there was a lack of virtues that, to me, are inherent in the axe itself, like strength and fortitude, the simplicity of the tool, and its manual function.

Soon enough, they started selling. I realized that it was a chance for me to seize this as an opportunity. Not only to reach out to people and spread a message but also to start a business for myself that could sustain me, and hopefully sustain others who feel the same way about beautifully made products. We spent about two years developing that axe and more recently, we've branched out and started selling other beautiful products—most of which are designed by us, and some that we could just never top. So we're also working with other great makers of things.

Early on, we realized that there is an abundance of beautiful old axes, especially the axe head. Those last a very long time. At the turn of the last century, there were three hundred axe makers in this country, all of them making thousands and thousands of axes, so there are a lot of them still out there. They're made better than most axes you'd find today. If people are going to own and use an axe, we want them to have the best tool that they can get. So we started steering them toward these old axes on eBay, where you can find a beautifully made axe for twelve dollars. But you have to put time into it, to recondition and refurbish it, and that's where the fun comes in. It's an amazing experience to bring one of these old tools back to life; they have so much character. Then to go out and actually use it, you feel like you built—well, you did—you rebuilt that tool. Then the owner has a deeper connection to it. So that has been a popular series: we'll go to different cities or locations and conduct workshops where people come and bring their axes, and together we sit down and refurbish these tools.

Everyone's talking about reusing things. It makes sense. Rather than go out and buy a new one, find something that's already there and with a little bit of hard work, bring it back to life.

## Anna Canoni, Woody Guthrie's Granddaughter
### Mount Kisco, Westchester County

Woody has these great quotes: "Don't swap this raw sunshine for too much stage light. The fight is here, lots more than on the stage." "The worst thing that can happen to yourself is to cut yourself loose from the people, and the best thing is to sort of vaccinate yourself right into the big streams and the blood of the people."

My mum is Nora Guthrie and she's always said that Billy Bragg is one of the few musicians around today who is most aligned with Woody—the fact that he writes songs for the message. It's not to be a star in the spotlight; it's to send a message, to open a discussion, to talk about issues. Using music as your instrument and to talk about things that are bigger than music.

Woody wrote so factually and descriptively about historic events and he was a wordsmith—which has helped him stay timeless. The issues are the same; it's cyclical. There may be different details, but greed is always relevant. So many social issues will always be relevant.

Woody migrated from Oklahoma to California. Going through that process with hundreds of thousands of people who were broke, had nothing, maybe a car, maybe some furniture, maybe, maybe, maybe... But never got an opportunity to sell their property, or their farm that they had spent their lives working on, to have any money to go with them. The dustbowl came in and that was it. No water. Everything dried up. So he migrated with hundreds of thousands of people—the largest migration in U.S. history—to California. Then illegal borders were put up by the California police. "You can't get in unless you've got fifty bucks, or a signed contract that says you've got a job." So there were these migrant camps outside the border of California.

Woody's plight created him. Your experiences create who you are. Woody's experiences were extremely hard and he became a survivor. Yet, what is so interesting is that his music, the words that he wrote, is so hopeful. Everyone wanted to hear him when they were down and out because he made them feel like someone else has been there, and we've survived it, and we'll survive this too. So everyone who goes through hard times can always find an in with Woody.

"Don't swap this raw sunshine for too much stage light." That's what he's talking about.

> I hate a song that makes you think that you
> are not any good. I hate a song that makes you
> think that you are just born to lose. Bound to
> lose. No good to nobody. No good for nothing.
> Because you are too old or too young, or too
> fat or too slim, too ugly or too this, or too that.
> Songs that run you down or poke fun at you on
> account of your bad luck, or hard traveling.

> I am out to fight those songs to my very last
> breath of air and my last drop of blood. I am out
> to sing songs that will prove to you that this is
> your world and that if it has hit you pretty hard
> and knocked you for a dozen loops, no matter
> what color, what size you are, how you are built,
> I am out to sing the songs that make you take

pride in yourself and in your work. And the songs that I sing are made up for the most part by all sorts of folks just about like you.

I could hire out to the other side, the big money side, get several dollars every week just to quit singing my own songs, and to sing the kind that knock you down farther. The ones that poke fun at you even more and the ones that make you think that you've not got any sense at all. But I decided a long time ago that I'd starve to death before I'd sing any such songs as that.

Your radio waves, and your movies, and your jukeboxes, and your songbooks are already loaded down and running over with no good songs as that anyhow.

My name is Anna Canoni, and that was written by my grandfather Woody Guthrie.

## Ted Ludwiczak, Sculptor
### Haverstraw, Rockland County

Ted, last name kind of a Slavic-Polish name, Ludwiczak. This is, we call it, Dutchtown, part of Haverstraw, kind of a historical place.

I've lived here for thirty-three years. The house was the best buy of my life. I used to own the optical lab in Mount Vernon, and when I reached fifty-nine, I quit, sold the business, and moved.

There are abundant rocks here, rocks all over—the county is even called Rockland County. I looked at those rocks and they looked at me and we connected. I saw some spirit, souls in them, and I kept carving for the fun of it. Most of them, they have a face; they're hiding. So I figure, if I peel it, I'll expose the face. And I achieve a certain amount of success. People ask me, "Do you see something?" Usually I look at the new rock, I keep moving him around, and I find a face. It takes me a couple of days.

Years back, we had a lot of storms. Those storms kept coming from Florida, traveling along the coast of the United States and did a lot of damage here. So one day I decided to protect my shoreline. I had the stone; all I needed was cement. So, I brought bags of cement, mixed it with water, and built a retaining wall. Took me a whole summer. When I finished, I congratulated myself. I looked at the wall, but it seemed like it was missing something. I still had some leftover rocks. One of them was kind of familiar. I looked at him; I kept turning him over and he looked at me. I found an eye, half a nose, half a lip, so I figured I'd add the other half. When I finished, I felt quite good. I cemented him right in the middle of the retaining wall. Next day I was curious if he was still there; maybe he disappeared overnight. I looked at him, he seemed kind of—the other day he was happier—kind of sad. I just imagined asking him what's the matter, and I knew right away: he needed a companion! First I gave him another one, and through that summer I gave him the company of forty. So the family grew to forty heads. Summer was over, and I couldn't stop carving. I built myself a shop on the side of the house, and I haven't stopped since. That was 1988, so I've carved over one thousand faces.

I used to work with chisels and hammers, but now, since I'm running out of time—I'm getting a little old—I use power tools. Basically I make a few cuts and then I chisel it off. I'm pleased. I rarely split the rock. Actually, I'm pretty successful. And so it goes, you know?

Children come with their mothers or fathers and suddenly it's, "Oh, there's Uncle Joe!" It's funny, because I left a big chin or big eyes. You can laugh, especially with the children.

I have visitors now, making movies, reports, magazines.... So I feel pretty successful. Now I can't stop, because there are so many rocks left here, they would be mad at me. I've got to keep chiseling!

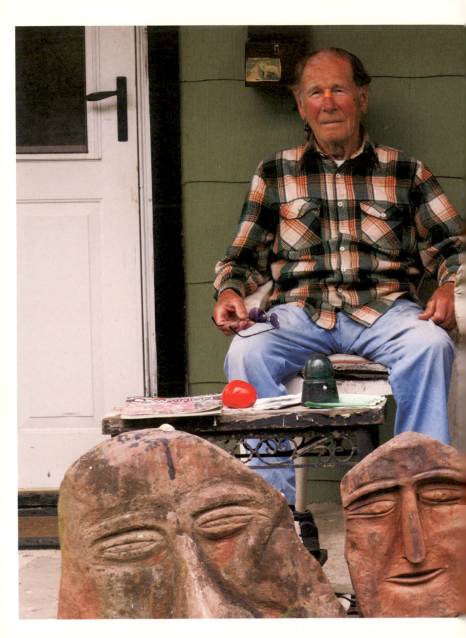

## Luke Ives Pontifell, Printer and Publisher
### Newburgh, Orange County

I'm Luke Pontifell, Luke Ives Pontifell. I'm a printer and publisher of handmade, limited edition books and a bookbinder.

At Thornwillow Press, our work involves the different related crafts connected to the written word, consolidated in one complex of nineteenth-century factory buildings. All of these crafts are under this one roof, starting at one end with the design, typesetting, and editorial processes to the plate making—where we make the copper plates and letterpress plates. Then, in the print room, are the presses for the books—we have engraving presses, die stamping presses for the stationery and for the illustrations in the books, which are often engraved. We also make our own envelopes for the stationery and our own marbled papers and paste papers for the books. In the bindery on the second floor is where the leatherwork, the gold tooling, and the edge gilding take place.

So our work starts at one end of the building as an idea, and it comes out the other end as a printed bound book that is handmade at every step, with the emphasis on beautiful design and craftsmanship.

I've been doing this for twenty-six years. I started in high school when I was sixteen, after taking a course in letterpress printing at the Center for Book Arts in New York. I printed a children's book, which was written by a family friend for her grandchildren, and sewed it on the kitchen table. I carried it to bookstores and asked, "Would you sell this book?" And they said, "No." I found a few stores that said, "Yes." In the meantime they've gone out of business! Then a family friend, William Shirer, a historian who wrote *Berlin Diary*, joked, "Oh, Luke, you should print something of mine." I was seventeen. He had this manuscript that he wrote about the dropping of the atom bomb and how he saw the world had turned at that point.

I did the same thing. I set the type by hand, printed it—one hundred copies—sewed it on the kitchen table, and carried that to bookstores. And then, every year during college, I made one book as a summer project. By senior year, what was a hobby had suddenly become this little business, and people were coming to work in my dorm room, and we were shipping out books. My poor roommate, I remember, had to navigate through these piles of boxes. The books slowly became eclectic in content and mixed in content, from books of poetry to short stories, fiction, and history. I did two books of short stories with John Updike, a book of James Merrill's poetry, Mark Strand's poetry, a lot of history, a book of Abraham Lincoln's letters.

This has been a dream my entire life, to finally bring all these crafts and operations together. It's almost like a little artisanal village, all together in one place.

We are committed to typography, beautiful printmaking, beautiful paper, beautiful binding—and bringing that craftsmanship and design together with interesting texts and manuscripts. This notion of preserving certain inspirations, whether it's a short story, a work of fiction, a historic document, a manuscript, to present it in a format that is beautiful, that will last, that will be here for readers yet unborn, becomes philosophically meaningful.

The book as a medium for communicating ideas has lasted longer than anything. Everyone says the book is dead; the *Yellow Pages* may be dead, but the book certainly isn't.

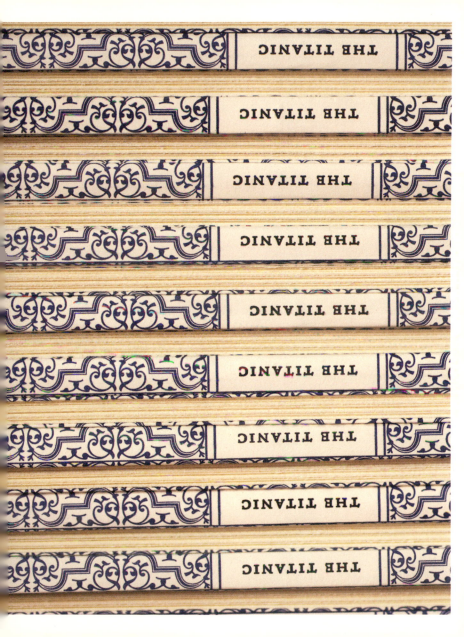

## Timothy Ganon, Yurt Owner
### Accord, Ulster County

I'm Timothy Ganon in Accord, New York.

My wife and I were interested in the idea of a circular building on the hill, so we purchased a yurt seven years ago. The yurt is a Mongolian structure. These are modern versions made out of marine-grade canvas and a lattice wall. Six of my friends and I went out and stood the yurt. I then purchased the trailer that houses the eight hundred pounds of batteries, 650 watts of solar panels, a marine ship-to-shore inverter, and the protective measures against lightning and ground fault interrupters. The trailer stands next to the yurt because you really can't put a solid building next to a yurt. They're made to withstand over one hundred miles per hour winds because the wind goes around them. If you put a solid structure next to a yurt, it blocks it, and then it's subject to the wind load.

We've hosted probably two hundred guests in the yurt from around the world. It's a playful space and operates completely off the grid. Last year, as I went down to feed the horses, there was a medium-sized porcupine standing next to one of my horses. You never see them out. I didn't know what to do with this porcupine. It was February; it had been a severe winter. I ended up—because he wouldn't leave the horse corral—putting him in a box in my shop and he lived with us for ten days. I could go in my shop and make a small porcupine noise and he would answer me. I could pet my porcupine—only rubbing him one way! I tried to feed him, and it appeared as if he was damaged by the severe winter. It seems he wasn't sheltered enough and he had some frostbite. He passed away after about ten or twelve days, which was very sad for me because he was a unique guest. I've had a porcupine stay for a little while.

## John and Janine Stockin, Maple Syrup Producers
### Accord, Ulster County

This is John Stockin at Lyonsville Sugar House.

Well, we pretty much collect the raw sap, which is usually 2 percent sugar, then bring it to the sap house. Right now we run it through a reverse osmosis that brings it up to about 5 percent sugar. Then we run it through a wood-fired evaporator, which reduces it, and the sugar goes from 5 percent to 66 percent.

I'm Janine Stockin, and I'm pretty proud to be part of this maple business. One of our maple syrup labels says, "Made in the Hudson Valley." It seems that this area, the East Coast, is where maple syrup is made the most, aside from Canada.

Fresh maple sap is very healthy for you. It's a cleanser. It has as much calcium as fresh milk, and it's high in vitamin B and high in specific minerals.

On our five-acre farm we have about seven hundred taps, which equals, probably, six hundred trees. Some are tapped twice. Our business of making syrup, in a two-mile radius of the farm, taps other properties, and we then extend our taps to about 3,500. We were at a 4,000-tap process, but we had this very strong hurricane last year—Irene—and that took away a whole maple syrup lot of 600 taps.

We mostly sell our syrup from our farm and at farmers' markets. We sell it right now—because of the amount that we make—in pretty much a thirty-mile radius of our community.

It's a tradition that's been carried on from Native American culture. The story told to me is that in the days of the Native Americans, they had only to gather this finished product from the tree. Now the

Native American story goes that we became a little too complacent about gathering that finished product, so we learned how to tap the trees.

In the history of many maple syrup producers, the family would tap the trees from the beginning of March to mid-March, when there are still freezing nights and days warming up to 40 to 60 degrees. This difference in temperature allows the sap to rise into the tree and flow naturally. So they were getting a source of sweet water, boiling it down, and carrying it with all sorts of buckets and taps that they made from trees. It's amazing to see the old technology. They would boil this down and have sweet syrup right from their backyards. And many families still do just that.

It's a product that people value as nature's giving, still. There's a camaraderie that comes from the family doing it together, or the individual, like John, who decided that he wants to make maple syrup. He loves to go into the woods in winter, tap the trees, run lines, work hard cutting wood to boil the sap down on a gross production level. This is his vision, his dream. It's like soul work or something.

## Deborah Ehrlich, Glass Designer
Accord, Ulster County

I'm Deborah Ehrlich. I live in Accord, New York, and I'm a glass designer.

When I'm looking for inspiration, one of the objects I return to over and over is this Masai spear. When I pick it up and put it in my hand, I can feel the speed. I feel like the person who made it.

I trained as a sculptor, not really as a designer. With objects, you can almost always see or read what someone is thinking when they're working. One of the most difficult experiences was studying with a teacher who could see what I was thinking. If I was self-conscious, he could read it, and a pure drawing would completely blow him away.

That purity is what I'm trying to achieve when I work. It's good to empty your mind and just enjoy yourself while you're working. That is one of the reasons why I do work, to enjoy myself. Designing physical objects is a bit different than sculpture. In some ways, sculpture can often achieve this, but I feel that sculpture can also encompass a lot of scarier and darker thoughts. With design, for me in any case, the way I approach it is to not address anything psychological or personal or intellectual. It's just this object that you hope will encompass the feeling that you have while you're doing it. Which is why it's so important for me that the people who are helping me make my work, and fabricate it, respect every small detail. At the beginning when I was starting out, people would say, "Well, you could make this for half the price if you just change this by, literally, one millimeter." And I would just keep that millimeter.

When people are experiencing joy, it affects everything. You know, it really does. It also affects, and translates into, physical objects. When I sit down to draw something, I will either pick up my spear and feel it, and be inspired by the person who put that feeling into it, or I will read, and reread, a section of a poem that I find incredibly beautiful, like a poem that was written for someone, which has a special extra something. Or a piece of music—my brother is a composer—sometimes I listen to just a few clips over and over again for a day. Then I'll try to get that—whatever that nebulous thing is—into this very simple line drawing. In a way, I'm translating and borrowing from almost everything. But that's fine. I have a relationship with these people or with these sounds or with these poems or with these objects, and I enjoy the process of being with them 100 percent, for hours and hours and hours.

When I designed the thin decanter, I was looking at the spear. I tried to get the weight right; I tried to make it so that when you picked it up, you wanted to pour it. I tried to get it to look like it might fly right off the table. There's no other way to do it than to believe that it's going to fly right off the table. It's really just an act of faith. Glass is a magical material, and it has particularities that I don't necessarily know all about. I can guess at them, but would I know that this angle is impossible to make versus a slightly different angle, which is so easy to make? I wouldn't know until the craftsman tells me. It's such a pleasure working with craftsmen. If you're having difficulties, you're experiencing them together, because you're trying to create something beautiful.

## Ken Greene, Seed Librarian
### Accord, Ulster County

I'm Ken Greene, and we're at the Seed Library farm, our home.

I was working at a small town library, just over the Shawangunk Ridge from here. It was a book library, a public library, and I was learning a lot about issues, in terms of the loss of genetic diversity, consolidation of seed resources, while my garden was getting bigger every year. So I started learning how to save seeds, as a way of feeling that I can actually do something about these problems myself. But I didn't really feel like it was enough. So I thought, "Well, we have this great library system already in place. Kind of a radically democratic institution." It seemed like a good way of sharing seeds with other gardeners. So I added seeds to the library catalog. People could come in, check them out like a book, grow them in their garden, eat, pick flowers, whatever, as long as they saved some seeds from their plants to return to the library. The goal was to make sure varieties with regional history or varieties that are regionally adapted to the Northeast would stay adapted and wouldn't disappear.

It just grew from there and eventually my partner Doug and I quit our jobs. None of us could afford land—in this area it's pretty expensive—so by pooling our resources, a group of us were able to buy this place. That first building, the boarding house, we fixed up together and we all lived there for a couple of years while we were starting to figure out what we were going to do with the rest of the buildings. Doug and I built the cabin up there, and that's where we live now. The hotel and the mess hall are too far gone to save, but they're also too expensive to tear down and get rid of. So they're just kind of rotting for now.

We're establishing this middle field here as an orchard, mostly for ourselves, our friends, and our community. We've put in about thirty-five fruit trees, grapes, currants, and hardy kiwis—all kinds of stuff. Erin—she was a farmer before she started working with us—is always itching to come out and grow. So she's turning this middle space into a demonstration garden so that we can hold workshops here. People will learn about gardening, but also about how to integrate seed saving into the home garden, and see it in an actual home garden setting, rather than on the farm, which is a little bit different. The demonstration garden will also be our trial area, because we want to be able to grow, eat, and cook with them and know that "yes, this seed does really well here, and we love it," before we commit space to its production. So that's going to be helpful, the prerequisite for figuring out what seeds we're going to grow the following season.

All seeds have stories. It doesn't really matter to me how far back the story goes; it doesn't have to be a two-hundred-year-old amazing tragic romantic saga. Sometimes it's just the story of someone saying, "I grew this variety; here's why it did really well; here's how I used it; here's how I cooked with it; here are the things that I thought were important about this plant and why I think it's wonderful," and then passing it on to us. That's the story I'm interested in, as well as the bigger stories. Seed stories are always changing, even a seed that you might not think has a story because it's a commercial variety or it's been around a long time.

Part of what makes it so amazing here is that we're surrounded by woods. It's very private, very quiet and peaceful. I just…love it back here.

## Julie Hedrick, Painter and Poet
## Peter Wetzler, Composer and Pianist
### Kingston, Ulster County

I'm Julie Hedrick. I'm a painter and a poet. We're in Kingston, New York, in the Chapel Room, in my studio.

I feel very connected to the Hudson Valley, the landscape and the river running through the middle of it. I usually spend every morning visiting the river. Walking along it first thing, that sort of sets the tone for the day. I bring that quality and energy into the work that I do. It's a combination of grandeur and magic in the smallest details as well. And it's always changing. And the scale: I'm comfortable in large spaces. I like to re-create that feeling.

These canvases are abstract and they are very simple, but the feeling of standing in front of the Hudson River is what I'm trying to capture and bring to others through the abstraction of this color and the quality of the changing light. These canvases, they change as well, all day long, depending on the kind of light that's reflected on them. It's almost like they're living. I imagine—because I haven't had this exhibition yet—that when people walk into the gallery they are going to feel like they are walking into the forest, walking next to the river. They'll experience the light and the energy of that, there.

There's something about Peter's music—the composition and the feeling of it—and the composition and feeling of my painting. It's connected; it always has been.

I'm Peter Wetzler, a composer and pianist.

It's an exciting time for me. I write music for film and television, and I have a radio show called *Sound Forms: Conversations with Composers*. I also write music for postmodern dancers, more avant-garde electronic stuff. I'm passionate about the relationship between music and moving images. There's a wonderful relationship that I noticed in Balinese music and dance, and it struck me to the core; a relationship between movement and sound, this marriage of the two, that is extraordinary—and that you never see in ballet and only occasionally see in modern dance.

I really stopped performing solo piano over twenty years ago, though I continued performing with an ensemble called The Repeatos. While we all come from various musical traditions, we are passionate about free improvisation. We've done this for twenty years, but we're often not able to perform for long stretches, because it's hard to get seven people who live in seven different places together. Then this idea came up of returning to solo piano. You don't have to carry it with you, you don't need a roadie, and you can just show up and play. No trying to schedule around six other people. So I've been evolving this same kind of spontaneous improvisation on the piano, where I sit and I play the moment. First I recorded two CDs of solo piano music, then I had the courage to go out and perform these evenings of improvisatory solo piano live, starting with small parlor concerts and moving to concert halls in Toronto, Woodstock, and soon New York City.

I'm really loving it, because it's bringing together my classical training, the free improv, the minimalism, and all the film score projects that I've been working on. So it's an exciting time.

## Nick Zachos, Boat Restorer
Hudson, Columbia County

Well, my name is Nick Zachos, and we're in Hudson, New York, kind of halfway up the Hudson Valley, in between New York City and Albany.

We're here with the *Eleanor*, a historic yacht—a sloop—which sailed for many years on the Hudson River and is now in a warehouse in Hudson. It's ready to be restored as a not-for-profit venture. We're trying to turn it into a community project to learn about boatbuilding and boat design. Hopefully, we'll fix it up and teach people about sailing on the river and being on the river, which is something that's kind of disconnected from a lot of the towns on the Hudson River in recent years. Even though they're all right here, a lot of people don't have access to it and don't get on the water very much.

There's a little debate about when this sloop was designed. We think it was designed around the turn of the last century, early 1900s, by Clinton Crane, who was a pretty famous naval architect. The year 1905 was passed around, but some evidence may've come to light putting it closer to 1903. It would've been a racing boat. It's an incredibly sleek, long, narrow design, very hydrodynamic and fast. It's designed to turn very quickly, and to not draw a huge amount of water, because the Hudson River has some deep channels but, for the most part, there are a lot of shallow spots and you need to be able to tack in pretty shallow water. So it was designed for that, and it was owned by fairly wealthy families for the bulk of the century, who would've gone out pleasure cruising, or maybe even racing, on the Hudson River. I believe the family who owned it for the last fifty or sixty years used it as a family boat, and they would sail it up and down the river and go down to New York City.

At a certain point, when upkeep became a little too much, they decided that it should go to an organization that could take care of it, a yacht restoration school in New England. The school ended up not being able to take care of it and consequently defaulted. It came back to the family, who then thought of this idea—with a boatbuilder named Casson Kennedy—to try and restore it for the town and make it into a project that could happen here and involve the community in getting it back running again.

It would've had a single mast; it would've been a sloop, gaff rigged, which means that off the initial mast is another piece of wood that allows the sail area to extend more than it otherwise would, off of a typical single mast. It would also have had a jib on the front that would've increased its sail area. When it really wanted to have all sails out, it could have a decent amount of sail area. It's got a long narrow deck on top—that would've probably been a canvas deck—a very small cabin at the back, a little area that you could sit in while cruising. It definitely wasn't a pleasure cruiser. I mean, I think you could've gone and had fun on it and relaxed, but it wasn't a catboat or a wider boat, where lots of people could come and sit and drink martinis. I think it was designed to go fast in the water.

Right now we've got it partially sanded and scraped off. When we did that, we exposed three different kinds of wood used for the planks of the boat. It's double hulled, so there are the planks that we can see and, inside, there's another set of planks. The process that we're going through right now is very slow, but it's the correct and traditional way to fix a boat like this, which has probably been in the water for most of its summers, springs, and some falls, and then would get hauled out every year. When it would get hauled out, all the wood would dry out and shrink and cause all kinds of deformations in the boat. As the boat got pulled out and supported in different ways—and probably not all properly—the boat would've sagged at different points. Especially the long boat that we have here, the long narrow bow and stern have sagged over the years. You can see it if you step back. You can see that the bow and the stern actually sink down a good bit from the midship of the boat. In most boats along the sheer line—which is the line at the very top of the boat where the decking meets the planking—you normally see straight flat but often you see a smile in the sheer. In this boat, you can see a frown. You can see that it's actually unhappy and it's sagging.

What we're trying to do is to get an idea for the shape of the boat, in the traditional way of taking the lines off of the boat. We actually draw out exactly what all the lines of the boat are, like a blueprint for a house, except when you're doing that for a boat, you actually create what's called a table of offsets. You collect numbers of calculations of different parts of the boat in relation to one centerline down the middle, which then allows you to chart the entire boat. There are a couple of fun tricks that you can use to get close to what the original boatbuilder designed.

To take a boat that has been moving for a hundred years and changing shape, and try to get it back to that original form—if we can do it, that would be pretty amazing.

## Michele O'Hana, Ceramicist
Lenox, Berkshire County, Massachusetts

My name's Michele O'Hana. I slip cast tableware, in porcelain.

I create functional objects. I want people to use them every day and if they break, it doesn't matter. It's just a piece—it's not for Sunday best or Sunday lunch. You know, my chickens eat out of the seconds. I want every piece to function and multifunction. The pasta bowls can also be serving bowls, or they can be soup bowls. The drinking cups can be pencil holders. I really want them to be used in whatever way that works for you. They're not special, precious things.

I work in my own studio. I make my own prototypes and my own molds, and I mix my own slip. The beauty of slip casting is that even though the pieces should be identical, they're not. They each come out with their own personality, their own texture, their own thickness, and their own form. I work slowly; I like to take time on each piece. I wouldn't consider myself a mass production potter. I'm interested in how intimate the process is, how each piece really has had a lot of my thought, a lot of my time.

With porcelain, especially with these forms, glaze can be really distracting. For me, it's either all about the glaze or all about the form. I want my pieces to be all about the form. Because it's for tableware and food, I feel like the purity of the food is maintained because it's on a white background. If you were to put a piece of meat on a green plate, it wouldn't look like a fresh, nice piece of meat. It would look like a rotten piece of meat. With the white background, what you're eating is exactly how you see it. The colors aren't changed because of the glaze.

No fuss. No thrills. I think this is part of the Irish way. Ireland's not a fussy place. The people are very straightforward. What you see is what you get, and I feel that's probably the same with my work. I've never thought about it, but what you see is what you get. There's nothing hidden under that glaze; it's just the pure form of the white porcelain and the white glaze.

When I opened the shop and the studio, I wanted somewhere to sell my work, and I realized my work looks better next to beautiful breadboards or beautiful linens. It's enhanced by other people's work, so that's really how the shop evolved. Plus, I have a lot of friends making things and looking for an outlet to sell them. Why not all be under one roof? We're in the same boat trying to do something with our work.

It's a joy to come to my studio every morning. I'm surrounded by the state park and by other artists and craftspeople: chocolate makers, musicians, yogis—you name it, they're here. My surroundings are important to my work. It's a very intimate place, it's a small community, everybody knows each other, and everybody looks out for each other. There's definitely a secure feeling of being part of a community.

## Tom Crowell, Brewer
Chatham, Columbia County

My name is Tom Crowell, and I'm one of the founders, along with Jake Cunningham and Matt Perry, of Chatham Brewing, a nanobrewery in Chatham, New York, in Columbia County.

Five years ago, Jake got a call from Troy Brewing, where he'd worked in the past. They had a small brewing system housed in their barn, which had come out of a brewpub that had gone bankrupt in Albany. It was a relatively small investment to test the waters to see if there was room for another craft brewery in the Hudson Valley. There were a couple of breweries up in the Albany area, and then really nothing until you got down closer to New York City. So we thought it was a good opportunity to establish a new brand. We opened up five years ago and have found that there is a lot of demand and interest in our product—as there is for all things local these days. Now we're making ten different ales—still at a very small scale, a hundred gallons a batch. We're brewing roughly five days a week.

We worry less about being true to a particular traditional style, and more about making a beer that is very drinkable and enjoyable. Beers that we want to drink ourselves rather than what appeals to the mass market. We think that's a good recipe for success. To do that, we use very high-quality malts, and a lot of them. It's a more expensive product to make, but we think it yields a much deeper, richer flavor. At this point we are using a lot of imported malts from Britain and Europe. We're able to get hops now, somewhat locally. In the fall we do some fresh hopping of beers from small farmers who've started to plant hops.

Most of our beers are pretty much straight-up ales, and then we make a few beers, like our Maple Amber, which has become very popular.

We started it as a spring seasonal a couple of years ago, spring being the time when maple trees are tapped and people are making syrup. We added a generous portion of local maple syrup into our Amber Ale, giving it a little sweetness. We add it just before it goes in the kegs so the sugars don't ferment out.

I think our favorite is our Eight-Barrel Ale. It's a strong ale, with a fairly dark amber color and a lot of malt, so it's about 8 percent alcohol, which is where the name comes from. It's got a lot of hops but it's balanced, so it's not a true imperial India Pale Ale. An American trend is to make them overwhelmingly bitter so all you're really getting is the hops, but this is much more balanced, just a nice, full-bodied, rich ale.

All three of us started home brewing because of a love of the process. It's like we're alchemists. We're taking these raw ingredients and combining them in different proportions and coming out with an entirely new and different product.

We've stayed small; we're in Chatham, tucked away in a little alleyway, and people like stumbling upon us and bringing their friends and saying, "Hey, you've got to meet these guys." On Saturdays we have tastings and sell growlers—half-gallon, refillable jugs. It's really nice on Saturdays. People come back—if they know us, they always want to try what's new, and if they don't know us, they're usually excited to find us and try a true, small, local beer and have a chance to talk with our brewer.

## Steve Clearman, Motorcycle Collector
### Ghent, Columbia County

My name's Steve Clearman. We're sitting in what I call the Lower Barn, where I have my office and most of my motorcycle collection, in Columbia County, a bit south of Albany and east of the Hudson River.

My attraction to machinery goes back to early childhood. When I was a little boy, my father, who was a professor of physics, brought me to his work. There were laboratories but also a little machine shop. I remember standing at the lathe and just being fascinated by what the thing looked like. Pieces of cast iron machined very smooth and the warm reflective glow that it gave off. My father lifted me up on a stool and showed me how to turn a little brass bar. That was a magical experience.

Later on, as a preteenager, walking down the street in Port Washington, New York, where there was a famous motorcycle shop called Ghost Motorcycles, I remember looking up at the window and seeing a Vincent. The Vincent is a very impressive piece of machinery. It's quite unusual looking and very muscular, with painted, polished aluminum and rough surfaces and stainless steel bits. It was just the most beautiful thing I'd ever seen. That's when I thought, "Motorcycles are great; I gotta get a motorcycle someday." Which I did, later on.

I first saw this bike when I was on a ride in Death Valley. It's an old Indian, a 1938 Indian Chief. A fellow from Southern California named Stuart, an acquaintance of somebody I know down there, owned this bike. Stuart was a real old-time biker. He led a very marginal life economically and he looked the part: he was large, disheveled, a very nice guy. What I loved about the bike was that it was a highly functional, old, old thing. He'd owned it for a bunch of years. It had that barn-find look, because it was different shades of rust, a little bit of paint here and there. One of my favorite features is on the front fender: a bronze boat cleat, the kind you'd see on a small boat to tie a line to. How'd that end up on the front of this bike? Some kind of nautical thing. The bike worked, and I was thinking, "Wow, this is beautiful." The idea that it had been maintained mechanically and was fully functional, and yet it had forty-something years of patina.

Stuart, I guess, ran into tough times and needed to sell the bike. It was probably the only thing he had between, you know... starvation. So the bike got sold through a friend of mine to somebody else. But I kept track of it, I knew where it was, and a number of years later I had the opportunity to buy it. I liked the fact that this was Stuart's bike. He was a true biker; it was his life. It represents an image of a particular guy's life. To me, he's symbolic of the whole biker subculture, which doesn't really exist anymore in America. It was a little bit of an outlaw thing, you know? There was a time when there were a lot of guys out there whose lives revolved around their bikes. A lot of them were very nice guys, like Stuart, and some of them were seriously bad hoodlums. I look at the bike and I see what's there aesthetically, but I also see my vision of Stuart and what he represented in terms of that subculture.

The fascination with machinery, it's just something that's part of me and I've never been able to throw it off. There have been times in my life when I've said, "What are you doing with all this stuff? It's stupid. It takes up room." But I've kind of accepted that it doesn't matter what it's about. I get pleasure out of it.

## Lee and Georgia Ranney, Farmers
Ghent, Columbia County

**LR**: My name's Lee, and I'm one of the farmers here at Kinderhook Farm.

**GR**: I'm Georgia, and I'm also a farmer here.

**LR**: It's a diversified livestock operation; we try to have as many different species as possible, both because we think that they interact well and because it's fun. We produce local meat for the greater New York area and we try to make the farm a learning and community center for people interested in pasture-based and local food operations.

The farm has gone through quite a few iterations. It was, for a long time, a very strong dairy area, but that's sort of gone away as the dairy business has commoditized. Now its next iteration is a general breadbasket for vegetables, meats, and fruit.

**GR**: I think that people who are attracted to the place are interested in the visual aspect of it, as well as the nurturing aspect. It's an exciting place to be. It's always changing. We've finished lambing over an intense two and a half weeks. It's over now, so we're on to the next part of the process, which is grazing them. We work together to figure out how to move the animals and provide for them.

**LR**: The seasons are just part of the ebb and flow of the farm, like lambing is, or calving or making hay. The hummingbirds come back and the hummingbirds leave. The seasons are important, like all of the changes that occur during the year with the animals and the weather and the people.

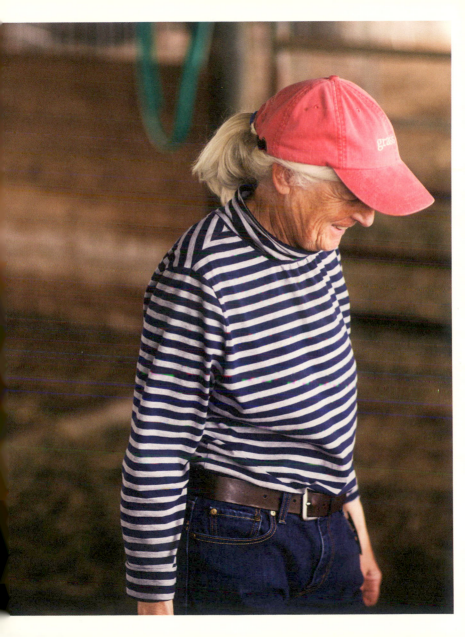

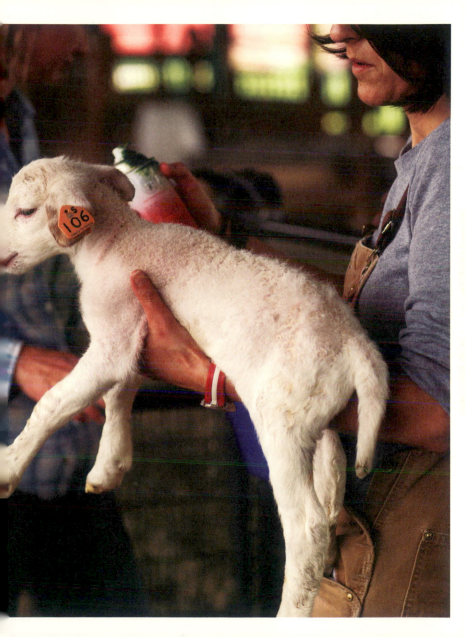

## Derek Grout, Distiller
Valatie, Columbia County

My name is Derek Grout, and I'm an apple farmer and distiller—more of a distiller than an apple farmer. We're at Harvest Spirits in Valatie, New York.

We converted this room into a distillery in 2006, when the laws changed to allow small distillers the chance to sell directly to the public with the understanding that they would use primarily New York State–grown ingredients.

When you have a still, especially back in colonial times, there would be excise taxes levied on you. The first national excise tax to be levied was for distilled spirits and it sparked the whisky rebellion in the late eighteenth century. But if you wanted applejack, all you needed was a barrel, an apple tree, and a means to press it. It was common for a farmhouse to have a barrel of cider outside. Old grandpa would open up the bung and put a drill, or a red-hot poker, into the center of the barrel to get that higher alcohol out. So if you empty this barrel, after it's been frozen, maybe only one-eighth or one-seventh of the contents of the barrel would be liquid, and the rest would be mostly frozen water. You'd get a thick syrupy consistency, almost like a port. So with one freezing, it goes up from 5 percent to 10 percent alcohol. We're freezing in five-gallon pails. We walk them into the freezer and the next day we take out the frozen hard cider, drill holes in them, tip them upside down in shallow pans, and empty out the more liquid, concentrated hard cider.

My grandparents started the apple farm in the late 1950s. They had moved up here during World War II from New York City and started working on various farms and bought this chunk of land. When my dad and mum took it over, I was two years old and had three older brothers.

I'm the fourth of five boys. That was in the early '70s. My parents took it over and my father expanded it, and he's been running it ever since. He's a quintessential proprietary farmer. He's gracious in so many ways and has encouraged me and allowed me to build this little farm distillery here under the shelter of the farm. We can safely say that we're one of the only places—or at least the only place that I know of—that grows their own raw material base ingredient for vodka production.

I'm proud of what I do, and I know my parents are proud of what I do. It's great to be able to find a use for these apples that keeps you here. The great thing about processing apples by distilling them is that, as you put them in barrels, they get more valuable over time. You can't do that if you make them into pies or doughnuts or keep them fresh. You know, there may be barrels that we're putting away here that my son, or possibly grandson, might crack as a fifty-year-old cask. Who knows what will happen to this farm in fifty years? One thing for sure is that alcohol, as long as it's in that cask, and as long as nobody drops the cask, will stay there. It'll evaporate a little bit over time, getting better year after year. It's fantastic, almost magical.

There's an aesthetic here—the way the light comes in, in the morning. It smells a certain way, like musty apples and oak and a tinge of sharp alcohol. It's exciting. Making it is really the best part. Right now we're bottling two-year-old applejack, but I'd love to have five-year-old or seven-year-old. Oh my God! Eighteen-year-old applejack? By the time I'm an old man, I can have some eighteen-year-old applejack that I'm truly proud of. There aren't many things you can make that get better with time.

## Jordan Fruchter, Mosaicist
### Schuylerville, Saratoga County

My name is Jordan Fruchter, and we're in the Canal Crossing Mosaic Workshop, in Schuylerville, New York. I'm a part-time mosaicist and a full-time financial planner.

This is one of the many workshops that we offer. We have a print shop down a couple of blocks; upstairs, eventually, we're going to have a fiber arts studio, a stained glass studio, and watercolor and painting. Geri Bowden runs the school. This summer will be the first mosaic workshop—we have three classes scheduled. Eventually we're going to offer classes for the print school, and we'll have other art classes as well.

About two or three years ago I took my first mosaic class. I've always liked art; I did it in high school but I never stuck with it. The class started and I was just really interested in mosaic. I like the order to it. I'm a very type A personality; I work a lot with numbers, and I can see the patterns and the order to mosaic. It's interesting, you wouldn't think of mosaic art as mathematical, but I actually see a lot of math in my art. So I find it very interesting that I'm calculating angles and writing numbers down. It's kind of a nice transition. People look at me puzzled and say, "You enjoy art?" and I say, "Yeah, I enjoy art because I enjoy math."

For me, it's very peaceful. The job I do full-time, financial planning, can be very stressful. Here I can work with my hands and there's a peace to it. I come down on a beautiful Sunday, drink a cup of coffee, listen to a bit of music, and work for a couple of hours. It's a nice release.

## Carole Foster, Spinner
### Northumberland, Saratoga County

I'm Carole Foster, and we live in the town of Northumberland. We have a sheep farm. I'm a spinner and I'm learning to be a weaver.

When I first learned to spin, my kids were young and after the hectic morning—feed them, get them on the school bus—I would sit down and spin for a while and just enjoy that time. I love teaching people to spin, so people come and we sit here on the patio. They come from quite a ways, because there aren't a lot of places to spin. I love it because it's relaxing. It's better than therapy.

This is a Kromski spinning wheel made in Poland. It's the brand that I sell. I like them best, because they are well made and reasonably priced. It's very versatile; it does whatever you want it to do. You can fold it up, put it in a bag, and take it wherever you go.

I'm not a technical spinner, I spin by feel, so I don't have a certain style. I kind of make it up as I go along and it works for me. I dye my own wool and I also dye for other people. There's a mill in Greenwich and I do their custom dying for them. We use the kitchen in the old farmhouse as my dye room.

My sheep are Romneys and Wensleydales. The Wensleydales are new to us. I have only a few of them so far, but I love their wool: lustrous and long and wonderful to spin. The Romneys are from marshlands, so they do well in wet areas. They grow a beautiful fleece, too. Everybody has a different preference, but I love nice, long wool.

Mostly I sell to people who come here and have an interest in the farm. It's the history of the farm and the raising of the sheep that inspire people to buy yarn and take a little bit of that experience back with them. I put a lot of time and energy into it, but it's a labor of love. It really is.

# Index

74
**Michele O'Hana**
Ceramicist
LOCAL
55 Pittsfield Road
Lenox, M A 01240
micheleohana.com

38
**Luke Ives Pontifell**
Thornwillow Press
25 Spring Street
Newburgh, NY 12550
thornwillow.com

90
**Lee and Georgia Ranney**
Kinderhook Farm
1958 County Route 21
Valatie, NY 12184
kinderhookfarm.com

46
**John and Janine Stockin**
Lyonsville Sugarhouse
591 County Route 2
Accord, NY 12404

62
**Peter Wetzler**
Composer and Pianist
Kingston, NY 12401
peterwetzler.com

16
**Thomas Wright
and Joseph Fratesi**
Atlas Industries
333 Douglass Street
Brooklyn, NY 11217
atlaseast.com

68
**Nick Zachos**
The Hudson River
Historic Boat Restoration
and Sailing Society Inc.
hudsonriverhistoricboat.org

# Acknowledgments

I would like to thank the generous folk who have opened their homes, studios, and workshops to me, my bicycle, my camera, and my voice recorder: Pasqualina Azzarello, Peter Buchanan-Smith, Anna Canoni, Steve Clearman, Hunter Craighill, Tom Crowell, Deborah Ehrlich, Carole Foster, Joseph Fratesi, Jordan Fruchter, Timothy Ganon, Ken Greene, Derek Grout, Julie Hedrick, Ben Lavely, Reneé Ludwiczak, Ted Ludwiczak, Michele O'Hana, Luke Ives Pontifell, Georgia Ranney, Lee Ranney, Janine Stockin, John Stockin, Peter Wetzler, Beth Woronoff, Thomas Wright, and Nick Zachos.

To my friends Richard and Mimi Beaven, thanks for the help, food, and nursing (during an unfortunate dehydration illness). A nod to Bike Hudson Valley (www.roberts-1.com), a very useful cycling guide, which I followed almost to the letter. My love and thanks to my brilliant wife, Harriet, who embraced New York City for six months and was always on the phone encouraging and helping, and who has made this little volume look beautiful. Thanks to all at Princeton Architectural Press, especially to Kevin and Jennifer Lippert for their enthusiasm for the project, to Janet Behning for handling the production, and to Paul Wagner for his attention to detail on the design. Thanks as well to the brilliant Sara Bader—we loved meeting you in the little tearooms of Manhattan and you've been so supportive and helpful throughout this little adventure.

Finally, to the amazing New Yorkers who were so friendly to this particular Englishman on a bicycle. Whenever I was a little lost and got a map out, a car or truck would inevitably stop and a baseball-capped head would pop out and say, "Can I help you, sir?"

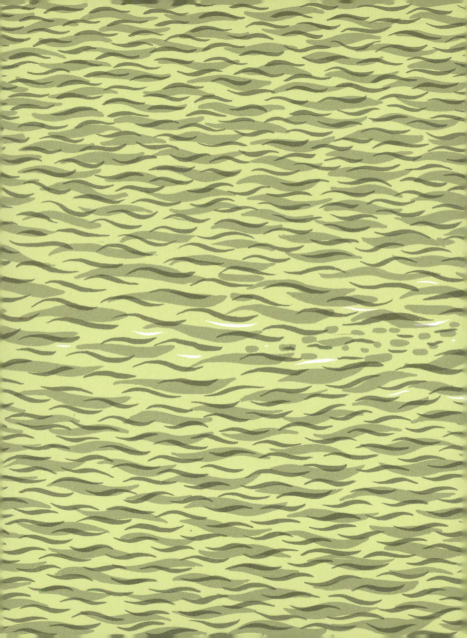